RE GCSE short course

THI
GOD
Teacher's Book

Maureen Harrison
Sharon Kippax

Collins Educational
An imprint of HarperCollins*Publishers*

Published in 1996 by Collins Educational
77-85 Fulham Palace Road, London W6 8JB

An imprint of HarperCollins*Publishers*

© HarperCollins*Publishers* 1996

Reprinted 1996

ISBN 0 00 322128 8

Cover and internal design by Andrew Jones

Cover photograph
Science Photo Library

Illustrations by
Mel Pickering, Contour Publishing pp30, 31
Alice Wood pp12, 13, 15, 27, 29

Printed and bound by Redwood Books, Trowbridge, Wiltshire

Commissioning Editor Domenica de Rosa

Project Editor Louisa Coulthurst

Acknowledgements
The following publishers, authors and agents are thanked for permission to
reproduce extracts and copyright material.

Adrian Brown and RMEP for the Hindu Game of Life which appears in *Skills
    Challenge* where many other games can be found pp10-13.
Christian Aid/CAFOD/SCIAF for the games Getting It Together and Slicing the
    Banana which appear in *It's Not Fair* pp26, 29.
The Guardian for the article on the Gulf War from January 22, 1991 issue p32.
The Mail on Sunday for the article The Awful Dilemma from July 16, 1995 issue
    pp24, 25.
The People Newspaper for the article on the response to Dunblane from March 17,
    1996 issue p18.

The following are thanked for permission to reproduce photographs.

The Mail on Sunday p24.
Topham Picturepoint p32.

Every effort has been made to contact owners of copyright material but if any have
been inadvertently overlooked the publishers will be pleased to make the necessary
arrangements at the first opportunity.

INTRODUCTION

AIM

This book is designed to support teachers running an RE GCSE short course using the students' book *Thinking About God*. It provides factual information, advice and suggestions for teaching the course. It also contains a number of photocopiable worksheets as a supplement for the students.

STUDENTS' BOOK

The *Thinking About God* students' book was written to meet the needs of the RE GCSE short course, in particular the NEAB Syllabus D Thinking About God and Morality. It covers the issues and questions commonly encountered among pupils considering the existence of God, religion and morality.

It was written with students of all abilities in mind. Exercise text contains questions grouped in threes with the first question being the minimum written requirement of students and the next two extending the more able students into deeper understanding and evaluation.

TEACHER'S BOOK

The teacher's book includes photocopiable worksheets for the students, and supplementary notes on some aspects of the short course to help the non-specialist teacher in particular.

THE RE GCSE SHORT COURSE

Using the student and teacher *Thinking About God* books you can run a comprehensive RE GCSE short course.

The first part of the NEAB course, Thinking About God, stimulates students to debate and discuss the philosophy of religion. Students will have the opportunity to develop their own ideas and beliefs whilst learning about a range of different views. They will learn that any response is acceptable if it is thoughtful and clearly argued.

The second part of the course, Thinking About Morality, involves the student in considering issues of life and death, relationships and issues of global importance. It will show students how religious beliefs can affect moral decisions. They will be challenged to consider the issues and draw their own conclusions whilst learning about a range of different views.

MEDITATION IN THE CLASSROOM

Meditation, or reflection, is an important part of the RE curriculum. It helps students to understand their own spiritual nature and therefore to more easily relate to religious belief.

The benefits of classroom reflection are well documented. Many students report feeling calm, relaxed and more in touch with their inner thoughts after they have spent some time meditating. The experience of meditation gives them the time, space and atmosphere to advance in their own ideas.

In *Thinking About God* there are three reflection sections (pages 20, 60, 82) which give students an opportunity to use meditation techniques. The following advice should help you prepare the class so that these reflections can be carried out successfully.

The role of the teacher is vital in classroom meditation. It is essential that the whole class is settled. The

following steps will help you to achieve a suitable atmosphere.

1) Make the students aware that they must sit quietly and close their eyes, even if they make no attempt to meditate. This is important, because if the pupils who are taking part think that they are being observed or laughed at by others, they will become self-conscious, and not enjoy the experience. It is often helpful to create a distance between the students to avoid distractions.

2) Dim the lights and draw the curtains so that the room is darkened. Students often feel self-conscious about closing their eyes and relaxing, and darkening the room can give them a sense of security and confidence that they are not being watched.

3) Ask the students to sit in a chair, keeping their backs straight, feet resting on the floor and hands in their

lap. Ask the students to close their eyes and concentrate on their breathing. Reassure the students that everybody is doing the same, and nobody will disturb them during this period. Then spend about 2 or 3 minutes tensing and relaxing each part of the body in turn.

The following words may be useful to help you achieve this relaxation.

'Start by becoming aware of the pattern of your breathing, feeling the sense of rhythm. Breathe deeply and evenly, until all your mind can focus on is the sound of your own breath as it draws in and out of your body.

Clench your toes tightly, hold them for a few seconds, then relax them. Feel how they are now relaxed. Clench your fists tightly, hold them for a few seconds, then relax them. Feel how relaxed your hands are. Pull in the muscles around your shoulders, hold them for a few seconds, then relax them, feeling the strains and tensions drift away.'

You can then begin the reflection itself. Read the words slowly, giving plenty of time for the students to take in and reflect on what is said. It is essential that the students don't feel rushed in any way.

At the end of the reflection, slowly bring the students' concentration back to the room. You can do this by asking them to concentrate on their breathing,

becoming aware of where they are, and bringing their thoughts back to the room. They can then open their eyes when they feel ready. This makes it clear to the students when the exercise has finished.

Following meditation or reflection, give the students an opportunity to share their thoughts.

- What did they think of the experience?
- Did they find it easy to do?
- Did they take part?
- How did they feel?

You could also ask the students to express their experience by drawing, painting, or making a collage. Or you could ask them to produce a piece of creative writing or poetry about their experience.

RESOURCES

New Methods in RE by Hammond et al, published by Oliver and Boyd, contains many useful resources and follow up activities for reflection work in the classroom.

Don't do Something, Just Sit There by Mary Stone available from the RE department, St Martin's College, Lancaster.

Anthony de Mello is the author of many collections of short stories, including *Sadhana, Taking Flight* and *Song of the Bird*, all published by Doubleday, that can be adapted for use in reflections.

RELIGIONS

CHRISTIANITY

It is assumed that before following this KS4 course, students will have a basic understanding of Christianity through following the Agreed Syllabus in RE. They should understand the basic beliefs of Christianity, have a good idea of the nature and variety of the Christian community and of how it worships, and should be aware of the significance to Christians of Jesus's life, death and resurrection. Students need to be clear that Christianity is a living faith in the world today.

Much of the philosophical argument found in section one of *Thinking About God* is based on a Christian belief system, although beliefs and ideas from Islam and Hinduism are considered.

Christian priests are usually willing to come to school to speak about their faith and answer any questions the

students may have. However, this can often result in the students getting a 'textbook' answer to their questions. It can also be useful, therefore, to invite Christians from other walks of life into school. For example, the local Christian Aid representative, a local Christian youth worker, or a Christian from a local hospice.

Students can devise a series of questions for them before they arrive which are related to the course. For example, they may wish to ask things such as Why do you believe in God? Why are you a Christian? Have you ever had a direct experience of God? Why do you think there is suffering in the world? It is important to make sure that the students are asking questions to seek opinions and help them understand a point of view, rather than to test the visitor or try to catch them out. At all times the visitor's faith must be respected by the students.

If the visitor agrees, video them answering questions so that you can use the video to stimulate discussion when they have left. It could also be used for future occasions if you have difficulty in getting hold of a suitable visitor.

RESOURCES

Christianity in Today's World (BBC Education) is a series of snappy, magazine style videos presented by Simon Mayo with a group of teenagers. They examine Christianity from a range of perspectives.

Exploring Christianity - Christian Life, Personal and Social Issues by Gwyneth Windsor and John Hughes, published by Heinemann, is particularly useful for lower ability students at KS4.

ISLAM

The central theme of Islam is that there is one God, Allah, and it is the duty of every person to submit to his will. Allah's nature and purpose for humans were revealed to the prophet Muhammad who recorded what he was told in the Qur'an. Muslims therefore believe that the Qur'an records the actual words of Allah. The other religious text in Islam is the Hadith, which is a collection of sayings of and about the prophet Muhammad.

There are five pillars in Islam on which the faith is based. A worksheet is included in this book which explains the five pillars.

Students could design a board game or card game based on the observance of the five pillars to help them remember the main points. It could be as simple as a snap card game or a snakes and ladders game where players go up the ladders for correct observance and down the snakes for negative attitude.

RESOURCES

CEM produce a poster pack on Islam which contains some excellent material.

Believe It Or Not made a very good video about Islam and the Hajj which is available from the BBC Schools service.

Gohil Emporium produce a catalogue of resources and artifacts available for purchase. They can be contacted at 381 Stratford Road, Sparkhill, Birmingham, B11 4JZ.

HINDUISM

Hinduism is a very diverse religion. Over the centuries it has adapted and absorbed ideas from other cultures. It is therefore difficult to define in clear terms.

There are many different Hindu religious texts. They can be divided into two main groups, the Sruti and the Smriti. The Sruti are writings that are believed to have come directly from God. Although they were passed on for many centuries by word of mouth, they can be traced back to people who heard them directly from God. They include the four Vedas – Rig, Sama, Yajur and Atharva – the Brahmanas and the Upanishads. The Smriti are writings that are human recollections of God's message. They include the Mahabharata, the Bhagavad Gita, the Ramayana, the Laws of Manu and the Puranas. In *Thinking About God* we have mainly used quotations from the Vedas, the Upanishads and the Bhagavad Gita.

Hindus worship many gods, but they are all aspects of the one God. Hinduism is therefore not a polytheistic faith (worshipping many gods) but a monotheistic faith (worshipping only one God). This one God is referred to as Brahman.

Brahman is the supreme, invisible, unknowable spirit which is neither male or female, from whom all life comes and to which all life will one day return.

Hindus believe that they can never fully understand Brahman – he is the supreme, invisible, unknowable spirit. However, to worship him they have to understand something of what he is like. The different gods represent different aspects of Brahman. It helps Hindus to grasp some of what god is like to personify him in these gods.

A good way to help students understand the concept of many gods in Hinduism is to consider the different aspects of a parent's life. They can think about all the different jobs of a parent: provider, cook, cleaner, leader, teacher, judge, counsellor, employee, discipliner, boss etc. Each role brings out a slightly different character in the parent and all together they compose what that parent is.

Brahman is neither male or female and therefore the deities (gods) can be either male or female. A male and a female deity are often paired together and accompanied by an animal which represents some kind of character trait.

Hindus believe that God is not just represented by an image, but actually resides in that image. Therefore, the statues are treated with great reverence. They are washed, annointed with oil, dressed in rich clothes and garlanded with flowers. Offerings of food are also made to them. At some points during the day curtains are closed around the shrine where the statue is kept so that the god may rest. The belief that the aspect of God actually resides in the image enables Hindus to have a personal relationship with God through worshipping the image.

Hindus also believe that God is all around them even though he is invisible. A story that is found in the Chandogya Upanishad can be used with the students to illustrate this concept.

> A wise man, Uddalaka, was teaching his son what God is like.
>
> 'Place this salt in water and bring it here tomorrow morning', he said.
>
> The boy did as he was told.
>
> 'Where is that salt?' Uddalaka asked.
>
> 'I do not see it' said the boy.
>
> 'Sip here. How does it taste?'
>
> 'Salty.'
>
> 'And here? And there?'
>
> 'I taste salt everywhere.'
>
> 'It is everywhere, though we see it not. Just so, Brahman is everywhere, within all things, although we see him not. There is nothing that does not come from him. Of everything he is the inmost Self. He is the truth; he is the Self supreme.'
>
> **(Chandogya Upanishad)**

It is important when learning about Hinduism to understand the caste system. A worksheet on the caste system has been included in this book and is related to page 33 of *Thinking About God*. At first glance the caste system looks like a social-class system, but it is more complicated than that. It is based much more on birth.

The caste system remains largely undisputed in Hinduism. Hindus believe you are born into a caste because of your actions in a previous life. Therefore, if your life is hard it is due to your own actions and is your responsibility. Therefore Hindus do not feel dissatisfaction with society if they are poor. In law the changes that have been made are to remove the status of untouchability, which is a level below the four castes. However, the practice in many areas is still to avoid people below the castes in order to retain religious purity.

There are advantages and disadvantages to the caste system, and it is a good idea to get the students to think about what these are. Playing the game *The Hindu Game of Life,* which is provided as a worksheet, will help them to do this.

To help students to understand Hinduism, it is a good idea to invite a member of the Hindu community into school to talk about their beliefs and way of life. They may also be able to tell some stories about the gods and give students a feel for how the gods help Hindus to understand the one God.

It is also possible to arrange visits to a Hindu temple. Students will be expected to remove their shoes before entering the temple. Enquiries should be made before the visit about any particular form of dress or head covering that may be required. A representative of the community may be willing to show how the statues are treated and how *puja* (worship) is performed.

RESOURCES

Pictures and statues of Hindu gods can be obtained from Articles of Faith, Bury Business Centre, Kay Street, Lancashire BL9 6BU.

Teaching World Religions by the Shap Working Party, published by Heinemann, contains a helpful chapter on Hinduism.

Teaching Hinduism 11-16 published by CEM contains useful background articles and teaching suggestions.

THE SACRED TEXTS

There are two sacred texts in Islam – The Qur'an and The Hadith. The Qur'an is believed to be the actual words of God which were spoken to the prophet Muhammad. For this reason Muslims follow its teachings very closely. It is split up into chapters called *suras*. The Hadith is a collection of sayings of and about the prophet Muhammad. Muslims use this as guidance on how to live a good life.

> He is not a believer who eats his fill while his neighbour remains hungry by his side. **(Hadith)**

> Make things easy, and do not make them hard; cheer people up, and do not rebuff them. **(Hadith)**

> I never prayed behind an imam [religious leader] who was more brief or more perfect in his prayer than God's messenger [Muhammad]. If he heard a baby cry, he would shorten the prayer for fear that the mother might be distressed. **(Hadith)**

> Allah does not look upon your outward appearance; He looks upon your hearts and your deeds. **(Hadith)**

> Your Lord best knows what is in your hearts; He knows if you are good. **(Qur'an 17:26)**

> Give to the near of kin their due, and also to the destitute and to the wayfarers. **(Qur'an 17:27)**

> Those that have faith and do good works shall be admitted to gardens watered by running streams and there they shall abide forever. **(Qur'an 4:122)**

> Do not wrong the orphan, nor chide away the beggar. But proclaim the goodness of your Lord. **(Qur'an 93:11)**

In pairs

1) Using the quotes above, discuss what characteristics a good Muslim should possess.

2) How would you expect a Muslim to respond to homelessness or famine?

3) How easy do you think it is to put the teachings of the Qur'an and Hadith into practice?

THE FIVE PILLARS

The word Islam means 'submission'. Muslims believe it is their duty to submit to the will of God. There are five pillars on which the Islamic faith is based and which Muslims try to follow. In so doing they believe they are following God's will. These pillars are:

1) Shahadah   2) Salat   3) Zakat   4) Sawm   5) Hajj

SHAHADAH (BEARING WITNESS)

Shahadah is the Muslims' declaration of faith. It says:

I bear witness that there is no God but Allah and that the prophet Muhammad is His messenger.

A Muslim will repeat this statement several times every day. They are the first words to be whispered into the ear of a new-born baby and every Muslim hopes they will be the last words they say before they die.

Bearing witness for a Muslim does not just mean saying the words. It means living out a life that shows to everyone what their faith is by reflecting their beliefs and values in everything they do and say.

SALAT (PRAYER)

Salat is prayer and a Muslim is expected to pray five times a day. Before they pray they must cleanse themselves spiritually by ritual washing called *wudu*. Each part of their body is washed three times with running water.

Muslims either pray in a Mosque or put down a prayer mat so that they are praying on something clean. They also remove their shoes before praying. They face the direction of Makkah (where Islam was founded) to pray. In a Mosque this direction is indicated by a *mihrab*, a section of the wall that is hollowed out in a curve.

Muslims follow a series of positions during salat (prayer) called *rak'a*, which emphasise their unity as a people and their equality before God.

Muslims also have private prayer which is called *du'a*.

ZAKAT (ALMSGIVING)

Zakat is the giving of a percentage of a Muslim's wealth to the poor and needy. Muslims believe that in helping the poor they are drawing closer to God.

SAWM (FASTING)

Sawm is the fasting from sunrise to sunset that takes place during the month of Ramadan. Young children, the sick, elderly, pregnant and nursing mothers are not expected to fast. As well as fasting, Muslims try to discipline themselves mentally to avoid speaking ill of anyone, or feeling angry or jealous.

HAJJ (PILGRIMAGE)

Hajj is a pilgrimage (religious journey) to Makkah, where Muhammad was born and the Islamic faith began. Every Muslim hopes to perform Hajj at least once in their lifetime. Before they can go on Hajj a Muslim has to make sure all debts are paid and their family is provided for. The Hajj is a spiritual experience through which a Muslim can draw closer to God. The Muslim on Hajj experiences equality and unity with other Muslims.

On your own

Draw a diagram representing the five pillars of Islam.

THE CASTE SYSTEM

1) **Brahmin** This is the highest cast group and consists of the priests and scholars.

2) **Kshatriya** The warrior or ruling caste group.

3) **Vaishya** The merchants and farmers.

4) **Shudra** Unskilled workers and servants.

Hindu society is structured by the caste system. There are four main castes (varnas) which are listed on the left.

There is also a fifth group which forms a kind of 'under-caste'. It includes people who perform menial tasks such as street-cleaning or working with leather. These people used to be referred to as 'untouchables' because their work involved death and decay which could 'pollute' members of higher caste groups. Gandhi believed that the treatment of these people was unjust and renamed them Harijans (children of God). In 1950 a law was passed in India making it illegal to treat anyone as untouchable. However, members of this group still find themselves living on the edge of society.

CASTE DUTIES

Every Hindu has to perform the duties of their caste to the best of their ability. In this way they are acting in accordance with their *dharma* (religious duty). For example, the duty of a warrior is to fight and defend what is just and true and the duty of a merchant is to trade honestly and fairly to the best of their ability. Every Hindu also has a personal dharma to perform. For example, the dharma of a father is to provide for his family.

If a Hindu performs their dharma well, they will acquire *karma* (merit). The more karma they acquire the more likely they are to move up to a higher caste at rebirth and the closer they are to becoming spiritually pure. The purer a soul becomes, the more likely it is that it will achieve Moksha (release from the cycle of life, death and rebirth, and reunion with God). The ultimate dharma of a Hindu is to achieve Moksha. If a Hindu does not fulfil their dharma they will acquire *pap* (sin). This means that at rebirth they will enter a lower caste and will be further away from Moksha.

Hindus do not generally mix with those from lower castes as they believe this affects their purity. For instance, it is forbidden to eat with members of a lower caste group.

The caste of a Hindu is passed on through birth and is not necessarily linked to wealth. A Hindu may belong to the Brahmin caste even though their family is poor or belong to the Shudra caste even though their family is rich. Regardless of the situation, the Shudra are expected to show reverence to the Brahmin.

> The responsibilities to which a brahmin is born, based on his nature, are self-control, tranquillity, purity of heart, patience, humility, learning, austerity, wisdom, and faith.
>
> The qualities of a kshatriya, based on his nature, are courage, strength, fortitude, dexterity, generosity, leadership and the firm resolve never to retreat from battle. The occupations suitable for a vaishya are agriculture, dairying and trade. The proper work of a shudra is service.
>
> By devotion to one's own particular duty, everyone can attain perfection. Let me tell you how. By performing his own work, one worships the Creator who dwells in every creature. Such worship brings that person to fulfilment.'
>
> **(Bhagavad Gita 18:42-47)**

In Groups

1) Discuss how a Brahmin might defend the caste system.

2) What objections might a young Hindu in Britain have to the caste system? How might parents help their children to understand its meaning and significance?

3) Play *The Hindu Game of Life*. What did you learn from this about the experience of being a member of a caste group?

THE HINDU GAME OF LIFE

Devised by Adrian Brown for 2-4 players

AIM

To reach Moksha (freedom from the cycle of rebirth, and union with God).

RULES

1) Each player has two counters of the same colour.

   One counter is used for keeping your karma score by moving it left and right on your karma total grid when you gain good ($^+$) or bad ($^-$) karma. At the beginning of the game this counter should be placed at 0 in the middle of your grid.

   The other counter is used for moving around the board starting at rebirth in space 1 and moving around the board in a clockwise direction according to the number thrown on the dice.

2) The outer ring of the board represents harijan, below the lowest caste, and the four castes (shudra, vaishyas, kshatriyas, brahmins) are each represented by an inner ring. The higher the caste, the closer to the middle. The centre of the board represents Moksha and it is the aim of the game to reach this point of union with Brahman (God).

3) To begin the game each player must throw the dice. The number will give them the caste (see below) and therefore the ring of the board they are to begin in.

   1 Harijan   2 Shudra   3 Vaishya

   4 Kshatriya   5 Harijan   6 Shudra

   No one in the game begins life as a brahmin.

4) Players must throw the dice in turn and move clockwise around the board the number of spaces shown.

5) Some spaces contain letters. If you land on one of these spaces, look at the key to find out what this means for you. Some letters bring good karma and others bad. When you gain good or bad karma, you must move your counter on your karma total grid either to the right or left to keep your karma score.

6) Players should keep moving round the board in the same caste ring (unless they are taken out of the human life-cycle by landing on a certain letter) until they land on the death space. At this point they should look at their karma total grid where they have been recording their karma score. Follow the instructions above the karma score for what your rebirth should be. If your karma has been quite steady you will remain in the same caste, if bad than you will drop one or two castes (if you are already in a low caste you may move out of the human life-cycle), if good you will move up one or two castes.

   Whether you move up through the castes on good karma is indicated by using the first letter of each of the castes. For example, H – S above $^+5$ indicates that if you are a harijan you become a shudra. If you are already a shudra or higher caste than you stay in the same caste. H S – V above $^+6$ indicates that if you are a harijan or sudra you become a vaishya. If you are already a vaishya or higher caste than you stay in the same caste.

THE HINDU GAME OF LIFE

KEY TO LETTERS

A Go on pilgrimage $^+$3k.

B Offer regular temple sacrifices $^+$2k.

C Help to build a temple $^+$4k.

D Give money to Brahmin (priest) $^+$2k.

E Do regular yoga $^+$2k.

F Read sacred texts regularly $^+$2k.

G Repeat 'om' $^+$3k.

H Feed a priest $^+$2k.

I Help scatter father's ashes on river Ganges $^+$3k.

J Say daily prayers in front of home shrine +2k.

K Offer prayers at River Ganges $^+$4k.

L Kill a priest, so reborn as a bull (move off human life-cycle).

M Steal from a priest, so reborn as a spider (move off human life-cycle).

N Lie to a priest, so reborn as a snake (move off human life-cycle).

O Neglect all family duties, so reborn as a bird (move off human life-cycle).

P Renounce Hindu way of life, so reborn as a frog (move off human life-cycle).

Q Go on pilgrimage at own expense, move to heaven of Vishnu.

R Build a new temple, move to heaven of Brahma.

S Sacrifice all worldly luxuries, move to heaven of Shiva.

T Neglect prayers at home $^-$2k.

U Use Upanishads (sacred scriptures) as firelighters $^-$4k.

V Insult teachings of Bhagavad Gita (sacred scripture) $^-$3k.

W Violate several laws of Manu (scripture about how to live as a Hindu) $^-$2k.

X Never learn to read Sanskrit version of the Four Vedas (sacred scripture) although an educated Hindu $^-$1k.

Y Hit a sacred cow with your car $^-$3k.

Z Forget to kneel in front of an image in the temple $^-$1k.

---

7) When you move from one life to another through rebirth your karma scores become

   $^+$1 if you have moved to a higher caste

    0 if you have stayed in the same caste

   $^-$1 if you have moved to a lower caste.

8) Some of the spaces contain letters which instruct you to move out of the human life-cycle on to one of the animals who are around the board. Move immediately to the animal. Your karma score becomes $^-$1. From an animal you can only move into the harijan life cycle beginning at the rebirth space. This is achieved by throwing the number indicated beside the animal.

9) Some of the spaces contain letters which instruct you to move to one of the three heavens around the board. Move immediately to the heaven and always remember which caste you came from. Your karma score becomes $^+$1. When you throw the number indicated at that heaven for re-entering the caste system, you should move to one caste higher than you were on before, beginning at the rebirth space.

10) Moksha is achieved when you have $^+$9 karma and land on death.

11) If you get $^-$10 karma or less, then you immediately drop one caste and begin at the rebirth space with a karma of $^-$1. If you are a harijan than you become a bird. (Let's face it, a score that bad is enough to kill anyone!)

12) If you reach a karma score of $^+$10 or more and haven't yet landed on death, then you can ignore all instructions that give you bad karma for the next life until you pass rebirth again. At this point your karma score becomes $^+$9 and receiving good and bad karma applies as normal.

13) The game can be ended either when one player reaches moksha or when everyone has reached moksha.

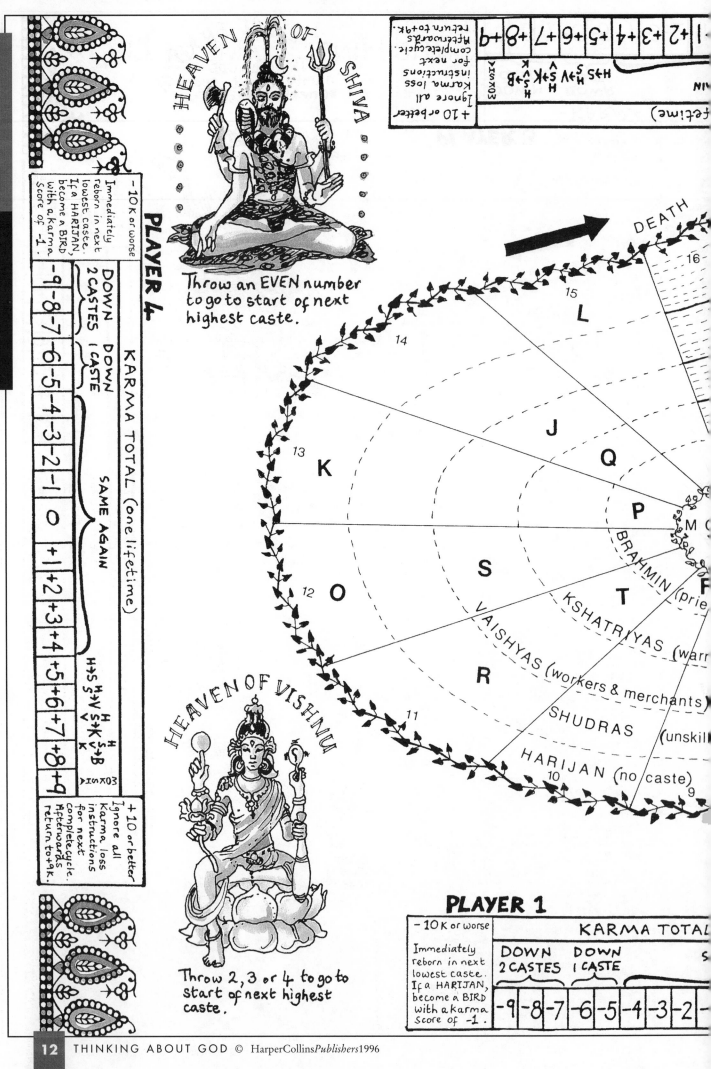

HEAVEN OF SHIVA

Throw an EVEN number to go to start of next highest caste.

HEAVEN OF VISHNU

Throw 2, 3 or 4 to go to start of next highest caste.

DEATH

L · J · Q · K · P · O · S · T · R · M

BRAHMIN (prie...

KSHATRIYAS (warr...

VAISHYAS (workers & merchants)

SHUDRAS (unskill...

HARIJAN (no caste)

PLAYER 4

−10k or worse

Immediately reborn in next lowest caste. If a HARIJAN, become a BIRD with a karma score of −1.

DOWN 2 CASTES	DOWN 1 CASTE	SAME AGAIN		
−9	−8	−7	−6	−5	−4	−3	−2	−1	0	+1	+2	+3	+4	+5	+6	+7	+8	+9

KARMA TOTAL (one lifetime)

+10 or better
Ignore all karma loss instructions for next complete cycle. Afterwards return to +9k.

PLAYER 1

−10k or worse

Immediately reborn in next lowest caste. If a HARIJAN, become a BIRD with a karma score of −1.

	KARMA TOTAL
DOWN 2 CASTES	DOWN 1 CASTE
−9	−8	−7	−6	−5	−4	−3	−2

+10 or better
Ignore all karma loss instructions for next complete cycle. Afterwards return to +9k.

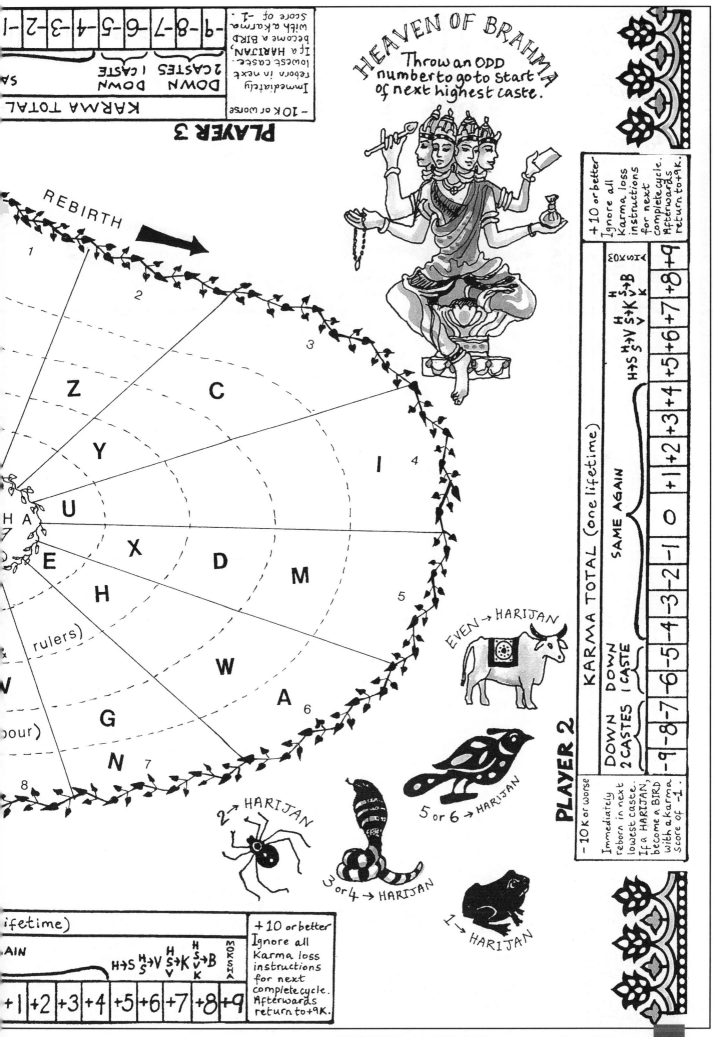

THINKING ABOUT GOD

Some of the philosophical concepts referred to in section one of *Thinking About God* are difficult to grasp. However, they can be understood at different levels which makes it possible to teach them to a group of mixed ability. For instance, some students may understand only that scientific theories about the origin of the universe put into question religious theories of creation, while others may be able to integrate the religious ideas with the scientific ones and think about the possible outcomes to this question.

EVOLUTION

The worksheet on Natural Selection relates to page 25 of *Thinking About God*. Evolution is part of the National Curriculum Science at KS4, so it would be useful to co-ordinate the RE work with the Science work.

This area of discussion often produces the most sceptical views from students. They accept the theory of evolution as fact, and will often reject religious beliefs on the basis that if the stories of creation are wrong, the rest of the religion's beliefs must also be wrong.

It is important to emphasise that the theory of evolution is just a theory, and while it seems quite probable, there are difficulties with it. Evolution has been supported by fossil records showing the development of species. However, there are huge gaps in these records. There is no evidence, for instance, for how birds and mammals emerged from reptiles.

The theory of evolution also depends on the idea that variations of species come about by chance and ones that happen to be useful are selected naturally. However, is it possible that complex structures could come about by chance? How could something as complex as the eye have happened by chance? This question relates well to the argument from design for the existence of God on page 24 of *Thinking About God*.

There are three main religious viewpoints on evolution:

1) That the theory of evolution is wrong. God created the earth and all species.

2) That the theory of evolution provides a rational explanation for the development of species but that at some point in the past God created the species that have been developed.

3) That the creation stories are myths which seek to explain *why* the world came into existence, not *how*. They are expressions that God is the cause of everything that happens in the world. The theory of evolution is therefore completely compatible with belief in God.

THE PROBLEM OF EVIL

The worksheet on Evil gives students more information about the different beliefs people possess about where evil comes from. Many students may be fascinated by the occult. It is important that they understand that getting involved with the occult can be dangerous. Playing around with beliefs about evil can generate fear which can cause anxiety, depression and physical illness. It is not known whether these consequences are brought about by some sort of force or are psychological affects. However, students should be warned to exercise caution in this area.

It is interesting to have a discussion about how evil can come about through a cycle of cause and effect. For example, if a minority group in a country are oppressed, then terrorists emerge from among the group. The solution is to break out of the cycle of evil. Religions try to do this by responding to others with reconciliation, compassion and mercy.

THE PROBLEM OF SUFFERING

Suffering is often brought about by things that we consider are evil – for example, the violent oppression of people. However, there is also suffering where the cause is not so obvious. For example, serious illness or natural disaster. The problem of suffering is covered on pages 34-44 of *Thinking About God*. The issue of free will is an interesting one that students can be expected to discuss. Is free will worth having? What would the world be like without free will?

NATURAL SELECTION

Charles Darwin first published his theory of evolution through natural selection in *The Origin of Species* in 1858. His theory was that species changed over a period of time by adapting to their situation. They adapted through the process of natural selection.

Offspring inherit characteristics from their parents, although they are not exactly like them. This means there is much individual variety within a species. Those members of the species who have characteristics most suited to their environment are more likely to survive and produce more offspring than those with less useful characteristics. This is called survival of the fittest because they are the best suited, or the fittest, for life in their environment. Characteristics that are not so suited to the environment will become less common and eventually disappear altogether. This is the process of natural selection.

Through natural selection whole species gradually change (evolve) over time. If a species did not develop characteristics that would help them in the changing environment, they would eventually die out.

Darwin suggested that human beings had developed (evolved) from apes through natural selection over hundreds of thousands of years. This was a very daring suggestion in a world that believed that God created every species as it was and that human beings had a special relationship with God.

Look at the illustrations on the left that show some of the stages in the development of a human being according to the theory of evolution.

 Group work

1) Look at the illustration and discuss the ways in which human beings have developed over the last million years according to the theory of evolution.

2) In what ways have the lives of human beings changed in the last 500 years?

3) What changes do you think will take place which will affect human development in the next 500 years? Think about the affects of environmental change (e.g. damage to the ozone layer), pollution, transport (e.g. wide use of cars), central heating.

 On your own

Draw from your imagination a picture of a human being 100,000 years from now. Label any changes you have included on your drawing explaining why you think they will occur. Compare your drawing with those of other members of the class. In what ways are they different? In what ways are they similar?

THE NATURE OF EVIL

We often wonder why terrible things happen.

Christianity, Islam and Hinduism all believe in the existence of evil and their sacred texts often refer to some sort of evil force.

There are three main ways of understanding the nature of evil: as a personal being, a psychological phenomenon or an impersonal force.

PERSONAL BEING

The most common references to evil as a personal being are Satan and the Devil. These are generally figures that are plotting against God to turn humans away from good. Evil is described as some sort of powerful creature with personal characteristics like a human being. Sometimes evil is described as a serpent, for example in the creation story from Genesis. Here evil manages to tempt human beings into disobedience to God. In the book of Revelation the Devil is described as a horned beast.

> There was a huge red dragon with seven heads and ten horns and a crown on each of his heads...Then war broke out in heaven...the dragon was defeated...The huge dragon was thrown out – that ancient serpent, called the Devil or Satan, that deceived the whole world.　　　**(Revelation 12:3;7–9)**

The book of Revelation also refers to a beast which can be recognised by the number 666. In Jewish tradition, every letter has a numerical value. The number 666 is the sum total of the letters which form the name of the Roman Emperor Nero. Nero was a harsh emperor who was responsible for the torture and death of many of the early Christian community. The reference 666 could be identifying Nero with evil.

AN IMPERSONAL FORCE

Some people believe that evil is an impersonal force that can affect human activity. It is not a creature or being but a force that can lead people away from good intentions and make them want things purely for themselves. For example, it may make someone desire power at any cost to others. This can lead to governments oppressing people to keep control, or the school bully terrorising their victims to keep their position of power. So evil as an impersonal force is a sort of unseen influence.

PSYCHOLOGICAL PHENOMENON

Some people believe that rather than a personal being or a force outside of our control, evil is created by human beings. It exists in our minds as a result of all the negative things we do or think. Evil is brought about by failing to show forgiveness, be patient or understanding. This psychological state takes us further and further away from God and creates a personal misery or hell. In this explanation, evil is something that human beings choose and not something that comes from outside of them.

In religions evil is given many different names and forms. They are all ways of explaining the urge that we get from time to time to do something we know is wrong. Religious people believe that through following their religion's teachings and moral code they can resist evil and follow the path towards God. This is the discipline of the Qur'an, the Bible and the dharma (religious duty) of the Hindu.

 On your own

Collect newspaper cuttings about things that you think are brought about by evil. Where do you think evil comes from?

THE CAUSES OF SUFFERING

Who is responsible?	GOD	MAN
A		
B		
C		
D		
E		
F		
G		
H		

On your own

Collect newspaper and magazine articles about as many different types of suffering as you can. Think about what brought about the suffering in each case. Fill in the table above describing the suffering in the lettered box and ticking either under GOD or under MAN for each case depending on who you think is responsible.

A Christian response

On 13th March 1996, Thomas Hamilton walked into a primary school in Dunblane, Scotland, and opened fire on a class of five-year-olds, killing their teacher and 17 children, before killing himself. The event shocked people throughout the world and they asked the question, How could this happen? Below are the responses of some church leaders to the massacre.

WHERE WAS GOD AT 9.30AM ON WEDNESDAY, MARCH 13TH?

FACED with the overwhelming horror of Dunblane, people cannot help but ask how could God let such a thing happen? That was the question we put to Church leaders and parish priests around the country. Clergymen and women of all denominations in Dunblane have tried to comfort families who lost their children, but even they admit that they don't have all the answers...

'I WAS in Dunblane on Wednesday and I'll be trying to share with my congregation today the continuing love of God.

'But I don't think the Church has any better or cleverer answers than anyone else, to be very honest. As Christians, we don't believe that God wills this kind of thing.

'I know that you could logically ask, "Why doesn't he stop it?" But that's like asking why are we not all puppets on a string.

'Jesus recognised that human beings could be depraved and eventually suffered at the hands of human beings.' *Rev Sandy McDonald,*

General Secretary of the Board of Ministry, Edinburgh.

'Sometimes I feel like saying to God: Lord, I'm not surprised you have so few friends when you treat the ones you have so badly.

'I suppose we make our own heaven or our own hell. If I did not believe in life after death, then the killing of these children would be even more horrible and pointless.

'But I believe that in their innocence and beauty they are now in the safe keeping of the Lord. That may be scant comfort for their parents and brothers and sisters at this time, but I hope it is something they will hang on to and come to realise.' *The Right Rev Gordon Bates, Bishop of Whitby, North Yorks.*

'You ask: Where was God? I can only reply that he was lying on the floor of the gymnasium in Dunblane Primary School with the murdered children.

'The Christian religion is a religion of tragedy, though it believes that in the long run, maybe in the very, very long run, love conquers hate and

evil.' *Most Rev Richard Holloway, Bishop of Edinburgh.*

'The Dunblane murders were utterly evil. How could God let it happen?

'The answer is that God did not make people to be robots. He gives us free will. He longs for us to love Him and love our neighbour. But this must be our choice.' *Archbishop of Canterbury George Carey.*

'Every person must feel shame that a fellow human being can do something like this. But if God had stopped those bullets, we wouldn't be free.

'Human beings are free to do loving and caring things, and they are also free to allow someone to acquire a skill for killing. So it's not only Hamilton who was to blame.

'We have authorities who approved his owning lethal weapons, knowing he was an unstable person.' *Rev Maxwell Craig, of Action of Churches Together in Scotland, based in Dunblane.*

'My Christian faith says that God created people with the gift of free will, and with any

gift it can be used or it can be abused.' *Roman Catholic Bishop Vincent Logan, of Dunkeld, Tayside.*

'It saddens me that here we are again. It's not so long since the Hungerford massacre.

'How many more of these are we going to have?' *Michael Costello, Baptist Minister, Sandbach, Cheshire.*

'My own niece was murdered last year in an arson attack, aged eight, and of course I asked the same question about God. I certainly don't think it's God's fault. I don't believe evil was God's intention when he created us.' *Karen Mackinnon, Parish Priest, St Mary Magdalene, Bristol.*

'The sun still shines behind the darkest cloud, so we can believe that God is still with those who suffer in their darkest hour.' *Rev David Anderson, Glasgow.*

'We live in a world that has turned its back on God. And what we see in Dunblane is a symptom of that.' *Rev John Bush, Plymouth, Devon.*

(The People)

Group work

1) Discuss the responses of the church leaders to the massacre.

2) What do you think about these responses?

3) What is your response to the situation?

THINKING ABOUT MORALITY

It is important that students have a good grasp of the definitions of relative and absolute moral values. These are provided on page 90 of the students' book. They should understand that someone can hold an absolute moral value on one issue and a relative moral value on another.

ISSUES OF LIFE AND DEATH

The first three moral issues that students are asked to consider in *Thinking About God* are issues of life and death – abortion, euthanasia and capital punishment. They are particularly contentious and many students may have strong views on these issues. It is important that both sides of the arguments are presented to the students. When using material from societies that hold a clear viewpoint on an issue, make sure that you make the students aware of its bias.

ABORTION

The video *Life Before Birth* explains the development of a foetus from the moment of conception and will help students to decide the important point of when they think life begins.

Some of the offices of the Society for the Protection of Unborn Children (SPUC) loan out models showing the foetus's development from 6 weeks to 6 months. They are detailed models and they come with teacher's notes.

The issue of the mother's right to choose is an important one and you may be able to get a representative from the British Pregnancy Advisory Service (BPAS) to come and speak about the mother's dilemma and decision.

Whether the father has any rights in the abortion question is an interesting point for discussion and may help the male students to become more involved in the issue.

You could try using role play to explore this issue. Try giving some of the characters religious beliefs and see how their decisions are affected by these beliefs. By changing the characters' situations (single woman, married woman with a violent husband, happily married couple etc.) students can explore whether their views are absolute or relative. The issue of whether a foetus that is handicapped should be aborted is also one that can be explored through role play.

RELEVANT ORGANISATIONS

British Pregnancy Advisory Service (BPAS)
7 Belgrave Road, Victoria, London SW1V 1QB.

LIFE
118–120 Warwick Street, Royal Leamington Spa, CV32 4QY.

National Abortion Campaign (NAC)
The Print House, 18 Ashwin Street, London E8 3DL.

Society for the Protection of Unborn Children (SPUC)
7 Tufton Street, Westminster, London SW1P 3QN.

RESOURCES

Dear Nobody by Berty Doherty, published by Collins Educational.

EUTHANASIA

There are regularly articles on euthanasia in newspapers and magazines which are worth collecting. Such articles will help students to focus on the issue.

We include one newspaper article which tells the case of two-year-old Ian Stewart.

Whose Life is it Anyway? starring Richard Dreyfuss is a film that deals sensitively with the dilemmas facing the patient, their family, and the doctors.

It is useful to consider the hospice movement as an alternative to euthanasia for people suffering from incurable illnesses. A representative from a local hospice may be willing to visit the school to talk about their work or they may welcome visitors to the hospice itself.

RELEVANT ORGANISATIONS

Age Concern
Astral House, 1268 London Road, London SW16 4ER.

Alert
27 Walpole Street, London SW3 4QS.

EXIT (Voluntary Euthanasia Society)
13 Prince of Wales Terrace, London W8 3PG.

CAPITAL PUNISHMENT

It is helpful when considering capital punishment that the students think themselves into the situation of the victim, the victim's family, and also the criminal and their family. There is some information in the students' book about the motivation behind punishment. The students can consider whether a motivation is acceptable. For example, is the motivation for revenge an acceptable reason to kill a criminal?

It is also a good idea to consider alternatives to capital punishment and whether they bring about a desirable result. What does putting someone in prison for a long period of time actually achieve? Is rehabilitation possible for a criminal?

RESOURCES

The Throttlepenny Murder by Roger J Green, published by Collins Educational in the Cascades series.

RELATIONSHIPS

The issues sex, marriage and divorce, the individual in society, and prejudice and discrimination are about how people relate to each other in society. Some of the students will have had personal experiences which relate to these issues and which may make them particularly sensitive to some opinions. It is important that the issues are discussed openly, but it is necessary to approach them with care.

SEX, MARRIAGE AND DIVORCE

It is interesting to discuss the differences between marriage in a religious building and marriage in a registry office. Does the location of a marriage make any difference to the sincerity of the marriage? Should people who have no religious belief be allowed to marry in a religious building?

It may be helpful for the students to find out what is actually said in the marriage vows in registry offices and in various religious ceremonies.

Understanding that religions view marriage as sacred is important in understanding their attitude to divorce. Many religious people believe marriage was created by God for a couple to share an intimate, loving relationship. They are united as one in God's eyes, and

therefore it is a holy and permanent union. Anything that tries to harm that relationship is going against God.

Ask the students to brainstorm the causes and consequences of divorce and use their ideas as a stimulus for discussion. You may be able to get a representative from Relate or a similar organisation to come into school to talk about the difficulties involved in sorting out marriage problems.

You may be able to get representatives from local religious groups to come into school to talk to the students – about what marriage means in their religion, in what ways they help couples to prepare for marriage, how their religion views cohabitation before marriage, how they view divorce, whether they accept second or third marriages – and answer their questions.

RELEVANT ORGANISATIONS

Relate
Herbert Gray College, Little Church Street, Rugby CV21 3AP.

THE INDIVIDUAL IN SOCIETY

The students will come from a variety of backgrounds. Therefore, they will have different ideas about the role of the individual in society. We are all subject to conflicting messages from parents, school and the media, so it is important for the students to reflect upon their own values, attitudes and opinions.

In the Christian religion, the Ten Commandments offer clear direction about how an individual should behave in society and following these commandments will enable them to have a rewarding relationship with God. In the Sermon on the Mount (Matthew 5,6,7/Luke 6 – here called the Sermon on the Plain), Jesus gives his followers a set of values that they should follow.

Islam places clear obligations on believers to treat others with compassion and justice. Through self-discipline, the Muslim learns the personal and community value of submission to Allah.

Hindus believe that the spirit of Brahman (God) resides in every human. The role of the individual is to devote themselves to *dharma* (religious duty) which tells them how to behave in their life and what their responsibilities to others are. Their ultimate aim is to reach *Moksha* (freedom from rebirth, and union with God) which is achieved through behaving selflessly in life.

The Space Colony game, which is provided on a worksheet, gives students an opportunity to think about the importance of individuals in the community. The game is designed to make it hard for students to choose couples without revealing prejudices. Their reasons for choosing some couples and rejecting others should be clear. It is important to make the point that all individuals contribute something to society.

The game can be extended by asking pairs of students to role-play the couples who have applied to travel to the new planet. Their characters will need to be developed to allow them to give reasons for why they want to make the journey, how they think they could help to establish the community and what personal qualities and skills they feel they could bring to the community. The rest of the group can prepare questions and interview the couples.

PREJUDICE AND DISCRIMINATION

An interesting way to approach this subject is to ask the students to think about all the ways in which people judge others. This can be a stimulating and often very revealing exercise. They might come up with ideas such as judgement based on looks, nationality, sex, wealth.

Another useful exercise is to ask students to collect newspaper or magazine articles in which they think prejudice of some sort has been shown. What is the prejudice in the article? What is the consequence of the prejudice for others? Why do they think the prejudice occurred? What do they think could be done to prevent the prejudice?

It is important for students to understand why prejudice comes about. The Judging Others worksheet will help them to do this. Trying to describe the personalities of the Mr Men and Little Miss when they only know their names shows students how easy it is to associate certain characteristics with people even when very little is known about them. References for the Mr Men and Little Miss can be found in the books by Roger Hargreaves, published by World International.

A way of personally involving the students and helping them to understand prejudice is to try out the following exercise. Choose a number of students in the class based on something like the colour of their eyes, hair colour, the first letter of their name etc. Do not tell any of the students what you are doing, but put a blank label on the students that fit your criteria. From this point, until you decide to stop the exercise, give them more difficult tasks to do, keep them short of resources and help to complete the tasks, do not ask them any questions and offer them no praise. At the end of the exercise tell all the students what you have done. Ask those who were given labels how they felt during the exercise. This can begin a discussion among all the students about how they feel about prejudice and discrimination.

RELEVANT ORGANISATIONS

The Commission for Racial Equality
10/12 Allington House, London SW1E 5EH.

The Anti-Apartheid Movement
13 Mandela Street, London NW1 0DW.

Christian Aid
PO Box 100, London SE1 7RT.

Catholic Aid For Overseas Development (CAFOD)
2 Romero Close, Stockwell Road, London SW9 9TY.

GLOBAL ISSUES

The issues wealth and poverty, war and peace, and the natural world are all issues of global significance.

WEALTH AND POVERTY

Most students will be aware of the great divide between the rich and poor in the world. However, they are often not aware why there is such a difference. It is therefore interesting to consider why people are poor or rich in various places throughout the world. Societies such as Christian Aid, CAFOD, SCIAF and Oxfam will be able to provide fact sheets which give information that will help you discuss the causes of poverty throughout the world.

Peters projection map and the Mercator map have been provided on a worksheet. Students are asked to compare the two maps, looking at the way the first and third worlds are drawn. When the students place the statistics on the Peters map they should see the global distribution of wealth and resources against the size of the countries.

It is interesting for the students to produce presentations in groups about things such as international debt, health care throughout the world, population distribution, education in the world, homelessness, and development projects. Information on these issues can be gathered from societies such as those listed on the right.

RELEVANT ORGANISATIONS

Christian Aid
PO Box 100, London SE1 7RT.

Catholic Aid For Overseas Development (CAFOD)
2 Romero Close, Stockwell Road, London SW9 9TY.

Scottish Catholic International Aid Fund (SCIAF)
5 Oswald Street, Glasgow G1 4QR.

Oxfam
Supportive Services, Oxfam, 274 Banbury Road, Oxford OX2 7DZ (for information on their work).

RESOURCES

It's not fair CAFOD/Christian Aid/SCIAF

Christians in Today's World, a video published by BBC Education, has a good section on materialism.

WAR AND PEACE

It is a good idea to begin discussing the students' experiences of conflict and to establish from this that it is often very minor problems that escalate into huge conflicts. Think about the conflict that is presently in the world and talk about what caused it (power struggles, desire for territory, prejudice, oppression).

The Gulf War worksheet relates to page 42 of the students' book.

Many students have trouble understanding and relating to non-violent action. They feel the correct response to aggression is aggression. It is important for them to understand the concept of 'turning the other cheek' or the Hindu principle of *Ahimsa* (not harming any living thing).

Not using violence does not mean being passive. Non-violent direct action can be a very powerful weapon. Point out to the students that non-violent action was used effectively in bringing about India independence in the 1940s, bringing about the collapse of Apartheid in South Africa and for gaining civil rights for non-white people in the USA. Stress that collective non-violent action is likely to be more successful than individual non-violent action. A useful analogy is school bullying. Against one victim the bully is a powerful and formidable enemy. When the whole community supports and protects the victim through their presence beside them and a refusal to have anything to do with the bully, the bully becomes powerless. Ask the students to try it and see!

RESOURCES

Gandhi directed by Richard Attenborough, produced by Goldcrest Films. (This is a three-hour film but it can easily be edited to make an informative 45 minute film about the philosophy of non-violent direct action.)

Contemporary Moral Issues by Joe Jenkins, published by Heinemann, has useful sections on nuclear war and non-violent direct action.

Ethics and Religions by John Rankin, Alan Brown and Paul Gateshill, published by Longman, has a good section on peace and conflict from the perspective of the six main world religions.

Scene Video: The Gulf War, published by BBC Educational, gives a full picture of the issues surrounding the Gulf War and considers the Just War Theory. This will help students in their discussion about this war.

THE NATURAL WORLD

Environmental issues are part of the Geography National Curriculum, so the students will probably have considered the problems of the environment already. Greater scientific understanding of the impact of human beings on the rest of nature has turned the treatment of the natural world into a moral issue. We have to make a choice about how we treat nature based on our understanding of the consequences of treating it in various ways.

The syllabus requires environmental conservation, pollution and animal rights to be covered. Subjects that could be addressed are the destruction of the rainforest, global warming, industrial pollution, transport pollution, endangered species (brought about by human requirements) and large scale farming (enclosed pens, injected hormones, unsuitable animal feed).

The environmental problems that we face are enormous and students can become frustrated by the size of the problem, the apathy of those in power and what they see as an inability to do anything about the problems as an individual. The issues involved are very complicated and students need to realise that there are financial and political consequences to dealing with environmental problems.

Students can be expected to identify a problem, see who or what is affected by that problem, find out what the causes of the problem are, decide what could be done to prevent the problem or reduce its impact on the environment, realise the consequences of the changes that may be necessary and the consequences of making no change.

It is often possible to get representatives from local environmental groups into school to talk to the students. Many leaflets and other resources can be obtained from the organisations below. Earthkind is particularly concerned with animal welfare.

RELEVANT ORGANISATIONS

World Wide Fund for Nature (WWF)
Panda House, Weyside Park, Godalming, Surrey GU7 1XR.

Friends of the Earth
26–28 Underwood Street, London N1 7JU.

Earthkind
Humane Education Centre,
Bounds Green Road, London N22 4EU.

RESOURCES

It's not fair published by CAFOD/Christian Aid/SCIAF.

Global Environment by Sterling and Lyle, published by Longman.

One Earth, Many Worlds by Roy Williams published by WWF.

THE AWFUL DILEMMA

AT first sight, Ian Stewart looks just like any other two-year-old boy, with his blue eyes, shock of blond hair and impish face. But Ian is different. Tragically different. His eyes can barely see nor his ears hear. And the only sounds that he emits are cries of pain.

When Ian was born to Bronwen and Jim Stewart on May 24, 1993, he was suffering from a rare defect which meant he had only one artery leading from his heart. An operation 20 months ago in which doctors attempted to insert a second, artificial artery left him severely brain damaged. Now he faces a life of isolation and uncomprehending agony.

Soon, his heart condition will begin to deteriorate. Because of the failure of the first operation, no further surgery will take place and his condition will inevitably worsen. At some point – maybe a few months away, maybe a few years – he will die.

Knowing that their little boy faces nothing but pain and an early death has inevitably led his parents to ask themselves the question: What is the best thing we can do for our son? The conclusion they have reached is that it would be best to bring his life to a close as swiftly and painlessly as possible through a lethal injection.

Their decision has brought them into direct conflict with the medical establishment. Euthanasia is illegal in Britain, and last week the British Medical Association reiterated that it saw euthanasia as unethical and members voted that it should remain outlawed.

Both the British Institute for Brain Damaged Children and Alert, the anti-euthanasia pressure group, yesterday condemned the Stewarts for their stand. But this family's terrible dilemma will tug at the hearts of any parent...and the lawmakers.

THE PARENTS

Why does the law make our son suffer?

FOR the parents of baby Ian Stewart the situation is clear. His mother, Bronwen, 36, says: 'What mother could stand by and watch her son endure a living death? He was once a friendly, sunny-natured baby, but now he is reduced to a tortured living corpse who screams and grinds his teeth in pain 24 hours a day. Why, when abortion is legal, when a mother has the right to end a perfect life, can I, as his mother, not end this damaged one?

'If there was any hope of a recovery, any chance of a miracle, I would pray and wait. But it's not going to happen.

'We must come to terms with the fact that Ian will never go to school, run a race, fly a kite or go blackberry picking.

'I know some people will look at me and say I only want to kill him to make my life easier but that's not true. He is in agony, sightless, soundless and terrified of what little he can feel. The truth is that my little son, the real Ian, died on the

operating table. My little boy went into hospital and this wrecked child came out.

'To kill him would be an act of mercy, not murder. I could live with myself knowing it would not be a lethal injection that killed him but the heart disease that has already blighted his young life.

'When the word euthanasia is used, those who are against it try to hijack the moral high ground, but there isn't any. What do they believe – that suffering is good for Ian's soul? They insist on the sanctity of life, but my son, as he deteriorates, will have no life.'

Jim, 38, adds: 'I view it as my parental responsibility to end his suffering. I know I would be branded a murderer by some, but in Ian's life he has known only pain and fear. Why can't I offer him this release? It is more loving and humane to kill him and free him from his husk of a body than to keep him trapped inside it. You would not do that to an animal, so why do it to a child?

'If I could give my life in exchange for Ian's I would. But I can't. I long to suffer in his place, but he's on his own. Doctors are always willing to play God when it comes to saving a life, so why can't they help us let this one go?'

The Stewarts, from Sidmouth, Devon, accept that those who oppose euthanasia have their hearts in the right place but believe they are fundamentally wrong. Certainly, as you see the care they lavish on their young son, there can be no doubting their love for him. Both gave up their successful careers as chartered accountants, and a globe-trotting lifestyle which has seen them live and work for periods in South Africa and Australia, to nurse Ian 24 hours a day. They live in a modest rented house near Sidmouth seafront on just £75 a week benefit payments and their dwindling savings.

THE AWFUL DILEMMA

BOTH say that if it were not for their healthy four-year-old daughter, Jessica, they would have killed themselves and Ian, such is their sadness and frustration.

Said Bronwen: 'Our lives are worth nothing to us. If we could have died with Ian, if the three of us could have gone together, we would have done. We would not have been scared to go with him because death comes to everyone. But we could never have left Jess. She is our sanity in all of this.'

It is almost two years since they had a proper night's sleep, a meal together or went on a family outing.

They admit Jessica's needs are secondary to those of her brother. A third child, an unplanned daughter, is due to be born later this month. The Stewarts both dread the future. But they make it clear they do not blame the hospital for

their son's plight.

They were warned that the chances of a successful operation were only 50-50. But they were not made fully aware of the risk of brain damage which occurred because of lack of blood to the brain during the operation.

Next year, the tiny implant in Ian's heart was due to have been replaced with a bigger artificial artery to see him through his childhood. Because the first operation was not successful, this will not now go ahead, and the couple must watch and wait as Ian's defective heart slowly fails. It is when that happens that they would like to end his life, swiftly and painlessly. Bronwen said: 'If you had told me two years ago I would have advocated euthanasia for a child of mine, and that I would be willing to do it myself, I would have been utterly shocked.

'But between Jim and me there has been a gradual realisation that it is the best we can offer him as loving parents.'

JIM said: 'I would do it myself for him. I would know when he was beyond anything and I would give him an injection that would put him to sleep. I would hold him in my arms and cuddle him until he died. I want to see a change in the law to permit some understanding of how a parent who loves their child could want to end its life.

'I would have great peace of mind if I knew I could do it when the time was right, without facing trial for murder. What has happened to Ian is heartbreaking and obscene. Euthanasia may be a crime but his life is already a punishment. Bringing him into this world was an act of love. Killing him would be an even greater one.'

THE DOCTORS

It may be cruel, but all life is sacrosanct.

MEDICAL authorities have already outlawed the idea of mercy killings for suffering children like Ian Stewart.

Yesterday two women opposed to euthanasia explained why.

Dr Peggy Norris, chairperson of the anti-euthanasia group Alert, said: 'It is our duty as a society to accommodate the least of our members. We can't just take the lives of the most vulnerable. No one, not even a parent, can decide whether a child should die. Life, in all its forms, is sacrosanct. None of us can determine the quality of life inside another being. There is a tendency to say some people are better off dead, but British law rightly makes no exceptions.

'It may be cruel, but it offers the same protection to all, and that is justice. This is the only life the little boy has, and he must be allowed to keep it.

'We sympathise deeply with the plight of Ian's parents, and can only say they must have more support

and respite care. But if they're allowed to go ahead with this, we must ask ourselves who will be next?'

Dr Norris added: 'Ian is not aware of any other type of existence, but we tend to put on to other people what we think they will feel.

'Ian's parents are obviously under a lot of stress, but they could consider approaching their own paediatricians for help.'

And, calling for more official help for parents like the Stewarts and their son, Dr Norris said: 'I do think the Stewarts ought to go to their MP. Unless we bring this to the attention of the authorities, nothing will change.

'Society will give support far less if doctors or, in extreme cases parents, decide if the baby is better off dead.

'We have got to keep putting pressure on governments to say we must provide more facilities.'

She added: 'The human mind can solve problems. We won't solve them by killing the patients. Euthanasia is a step too far. It would lead to all kinds of problems.'

Dr Norris was backed by Judith Rugg of the British Institute for Brain Injured Children, which has 20 years of experience helping such tragic youngsters to develop.

Ms Rugg said: 'It's incredibly sad but there is always hope. Children come to us nearly written off, and then go on to walk, go to normal

schools and play musical instruments.

'We would want Ian's parents to know that there's another option. We would be delighted to advise. This is one more thing to try. Don't give up unless you've tried everything.'

She told how another child who also suffered brain damage during heart surgery had been helped. 'He came to us in May 1994 and he is making good progress,' said Ms Rugg.

'We use a system which bypasses the damaged parts of the brain to get through to the functioning areas. Some results are little short of miraculous. Now the boy can run and kick a ball, his vision has improved to the extent that he can play with books and toys. Learning to speak will be the next challenge.

'We would plead with Jim and Bronwen Stewart to bring Ian here and see if we can improve his quality of life.'

Ms Rugg says: 'We ask parents to help us financially if they can because we are not a big charity. But we have never turned anyone away if they can't pay.

'Lots of our families organise fund-raising. The one thing here is how keen parents are to help.'

The Bristol Royal Infirmary, where Ian had his operation, refused to comment on his case or on the question of euthanasia.

(The Mail on Sunday)

GETTING IT TOGETHER

Divide into groups of five. In each group make five squares out of card or stiff paper (about 12cm square). Divide each square into three and label them in the way shown in the five diagrams below. Then cut each square into the three sections and place all the parts labelled A in one envelope, those labelled B in another envelope, etc. until you have five envelopes containing parts.

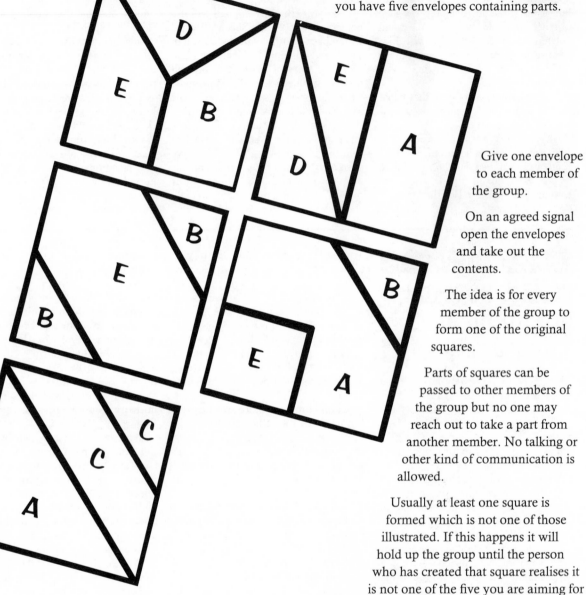

Give one envelope to each member of the group.

On an agreed signal open the envelopes and take out the contents.

The idea is for every member of the group to form one of the original squares.

Parts of squares can be passed to other members of the group but no one may reach out to take a part from another member. No talking or other kind of communication is allowed.

Usually at least one square is formed which is not one of those illustrated. If this happens it will hold up the group until the person who has created that square realises it is not one of the five you are aiming for and dismantles it.

The game continues until all members of the group have a completed square.

At any time during the game you can decline to take further part.

When you have finished playing, talk about the game. What happened? What feelings did you have during the game? Was the initial reaction of the group members to try and create their own square rather than to give parts to other members to help them form a square? What did you learn from this game about sharing and helping others? What did you learn about yourself as an individual? What did you learn about yourself in relation to other people? Is it always best to co-operate with others?

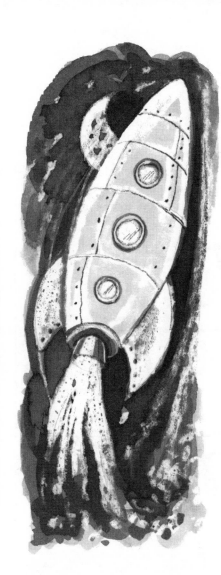

THE SPACE COLONY

Scientists have discovered a planet with a perfect environment for human life to flourish. The International Space Commission has invited applications from couples who want to go and live on this planet and help to establish a new colony. The space ship can only carry enough fuel to make the outward journey and can only accommodate eight couples. The only condition for the couples is that they must be young enough to have children, so that a new generation will be able to continue the work they start. Those couples selected will never be able to return.

The purpose of sending these couples is to establish whether it would be possible to have a mass emigration to the planet in two hundred years time. The prospect of global over-population makes this trip of utmost importance. It is essential that the couples are suited to the task.

Only twelve couples make applications. They are:

- Mr and Mrs Culshaw (Care Assistant and Housing Development Officer)
- Mr and Mrs O'Neill (Police Officer and Social Worker)
- Mr and Mrs Elliott (Postal Worker and Nursery Assistant)
- Mr and Mrs Jones (Nurse and Architect)
- Miss Hunter and Mr Watters (Chef and Hairdresser)
- Mr Phillips and Miss Blundell (Teachers of History and Technology)
- Mr and Mrs Howard (Christian Minister and Administrative Officer)
- Mr and Mrs Patel (Doctor and Community Relations Officer)
- Mr and Mrs Young (Farmers)
- Mr Jones and Mr Benson (Bricklayer and Plumber)
- Mr Madigan and Miss Edgerley (Scientist and Solicitor)
- Mr and Mrs Ali (Engineer and Dentist)

Group work

Select eight couples from the twelve who have applied to go on the journey.

- On what criteria did you base your selection? What qualities or skills did you feel were most important?
- What difficulties did you have in making your decision?
- What prejudices were revealed within the group? How significant were these in making the group decision?
- What did you learn from this exercise about the importance of individuals within the community?

JUDGING OTHERS

On your own

1) In the boxes above draw pictures of Mr Happy, Mr Greedy, Little Miss Bossy and Little Miss Naughty and around them write words that you think describe their personalities. Include things you think they would be good at, things you think they would be bad at and things you think they would avoid.

2) Share what you have written with others. Do you think you judged the characters fairly? What made you think they would be good or bad at things?

3) Why do you think we form judgements about people? Do you think it is fair to decide what someone is like when you know only a little about them? Do you think there are any dangers in doing this?

SLICING THE BANANA

Divide into 6 groups and name them growers/pickers, retailers, wholesalers, importing company, shipping company and packaging company.

Put a blank cut out of a banana up on the wall and label it 10p.

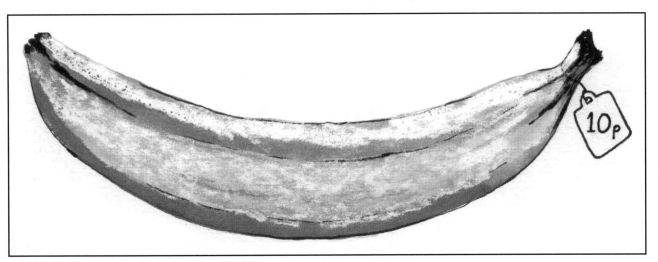

The whole banana is worth 10p and each group has a different cut of this amount.

Within each group decide what cut of the 10p you feel you should have, based on the amount of labour and costs that you think are involved.

Each group should present its case for the amount it wants to the other groups. If the whole amount of what the groups want comes to more than 10p, negotiate between the groups until the amount is reduced to 10p.

The actual cut between the groups is shown on the banana below.

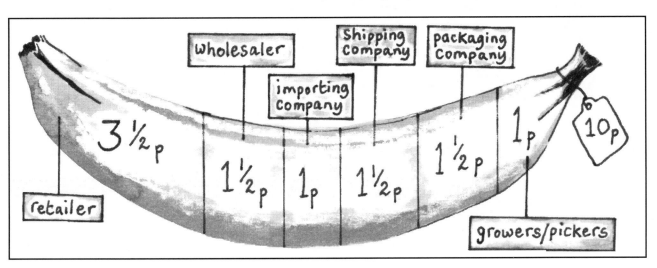

How do the divisions you have negotiated compare with the actual divisions?

What do you think about the actual divisions? Do you think everyone gets a fair cut? Do you think the growers/pickers get a large enough cut? How would you give them a better cut?

MAPS

The world is spherical, but on paper it is shown flat. To draw the surface of the world, it is necessary to alter its 'true' shape by stretching or squashing it. All maps therefore distort shapes or distances. For example, a map which tries to show the shapes of land areas correctly cannot also show the correct distance between any two points. Similarly, a map which tries to keep the scale consistent will distort the shapes of land areas.

The Mercator map below shows the true *shapes* of the countries, but in order to do this it has distorted their *sizes*, especially towards the top and bottom of the map. The line across the map divides the first world countries from the third world countries. The first world is to the north of this line and the third world is to the south. Because most of the countries of the north are close to the top of the map they are shown much larger than they actually are. The countries in the south are nearer the middle of the map and are shown more like their actual size. Therefore this map gives a wrong view of the comparative sizes of the first and third worlds.

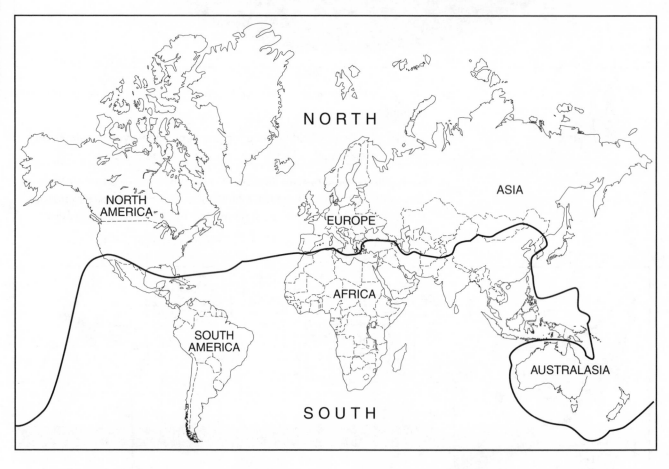

The Peters Map below shows the true *size* of the countries but has distorted their *shapes*. It is useful if you want to compare the sizes of different countries. Looking at this map you can see that the countries of the third world are quite large in comparison to the first world.

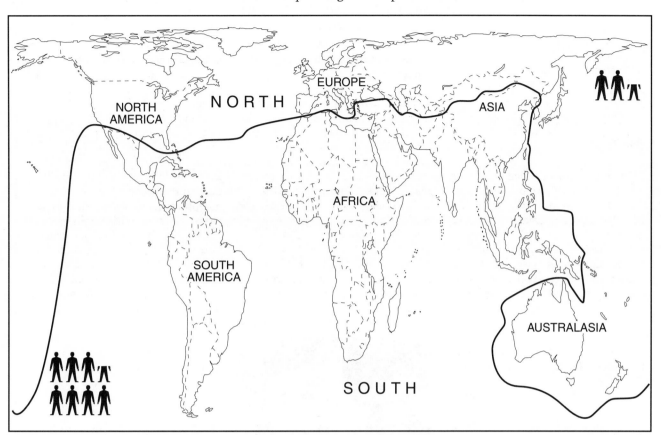

	FIRST WORLD COUNTRIES	THIRD WORLD COUNTRIES
POPULATION	24%	76%
WEALTH	85%	15%
GRAIN SUPPLY	47% (18% for humans)	53% (44% for humans)
PROTEIN SUPPLY	76%	24%

On your own

1) Represent the statistics from the table on the Peters map using symbols. Each symbol could represent 10% and therefore half a symbol would represent 5% and so on. Put the first world statistics to the north of the line and the third world statistics to the south of the line. Population has been done for you.

2) What does this exercise tell you about the distribution of the world's resources?

THE DEBATE ABOUT WAR AND PEACE: THE GULF WAR

Here both sides of the argument for and against going to war over Iraq's invasion of Kuwait put their cases.

The first American-led attacks on Iraq last Thursday [January 1991] confirmed what many had feared since Iraq invaded Kuwait on August 2 last year [1990]: that the long process of diplomacy would not prevent the horrors of war.

Months of international discussion, economic sanctions and the threat of war failed to persuade Iraq to leave Kuwait by January 15, the deadline set by the United Nations. The UN agreement allowed for the use of force to remove Saddam Hussein's troops after that date. Yet arguments continue over whether it was right to go to war.

Two main opinions have emerged. Some people insist that military attacks are the only way to ensure that the Iraqis are removed from Kuwait. The United States government, which has sent about 430,000 troops to the Gulf, takes this view. It is strongly supported by the British government, which has sent 35,000 troops.

Other people argue that sanctions, which block Iraq's trade, should have been given more time to work before it came to war. This view is held by MPs such as Labour's Tony Benn and Edward Heath, the former Conservative prime minister.

The case for war

PEOPLE who believe that it was right to use military force against Iraq have one main argument: they say that Saddam Hussein has used naked aggression against a small and defenceless country. He broke a basic international rule: that states must respect each other's territory. His action was morally wrong, and must be opposed.

If the world failed to remove Iraq from Kuwait, these people argue, Saddam Hussein's invasion would be seen to have succeeded. This could encourage further acts of aggression around the world.

In the late 1930s, they point out, Britain turned a blind eye when Adolf Hitler took control of Austria and snatched the Sudetenland from Czechoslovakia. Instead of stopping Hitler in time, Britian 'appeased' him and made concessions to ensure peace. This encouraged Hitler to invade Poland and led to the Second World War.

Saddam Hussein could become a second Hitler, warn people who back military action. He has threatened to use chemical and biological weapons, and to spread death to every corner of the earth, they point out. He also wants to develop nuclear weapons.

This is not just a British or an American war. The United Nations, which represents world opinion, has passed 12 resolutions demanding Iraq's 'immediate and unconditional' withdrawal from Kuwait. Resolution 678 allowed UN members to 'use all necessary means' against Iraq if it did not pull its forces out of Kuwait by January 15. If the coalition of nations had not acted on these resolutions, faith in the UN would have been weakened, as would its ability to preserve world peace. They further support the use of force because they believe that after six months sanctions against Iraq had not fully worked.

They also do not accept any attempt to link Iraq's invasion with the argument over Israel's occupation of some disputed territories.

The case against war

IRAQ'S invasion of Kuwait, opponents of war believe, was inexcusable. Saddam Hussein must withdraw, such people say, but force should not have been used so soon.

A war in the Middle East will have untold human, environmental and financial costs. Thousands of soldiers and civilians could be injured or killed, particularly from chemical weapons. They also point out that war could lead to an environmental disaster if Iraq were to blow up Kuwait's oil wells.

Opponents of war do not believe that the war will be short and relatively painless. Military generals said in 1914 that war would be over by Christmas. In fact, it lasted four years and eight million people died.

An economic blockade could have worked, opponents of war believe. Sanctions had already begun to bite. According to the American intelligence agency, the CIA, more than 90 per cent of Iraq's imports had been stopped by the time of the UN deadline.

The blockade had been costing Iraq about £41 million a day in lost oil income. There were reports that the country had almost run out of wheat and shut down many of its non-military industries.

Opponents feel that it is hypocritical for the United States government to claim that it had a moral duty to go to war. They argue that Western nations funded and aided the regime of Saddam Hussein in the first place as a means of resisting the rise of the extreme government in Iraq's neighbour, Iran. If Saddam is a monster, the West created him.

Some have made comparisons with other land disputes in the Middle East which have not led to a UN invasion. Israel has held on to land which it took from Arab countries in the Six-Day War with Egypt, Jordan, Syria and Iraq in 1967. A UN resolution says Israel must withdraw from these 'occupied territories', but little has been achieved to enforce this resolution.

The Western concern, many opponents of war believe, is ensuring that relatively cheap oil remains freely available.

(The Guardian, January 22, 1991)